THE FIVE POINTS OF CALVINISM

THE FIVE POINTS

OF

CALVINISM

ROBERT L. DABNEY

SOLID GROUND CHRISTIAN BOOKS
BIRMINGHAM, ALABAMA USA

Solid Ground Christian Books
715 Oak Grove Rd
Birmingham, AL 35209
205-443-0311
sgcb@charter.net
http://solid-ground-books.com

THE FIVE POINTS OF CALVINISM

Robert Lewis Dabney (1820-1898)

Taken from the 1895 edition by Presbyterian Committee
of Publication, Richmond, Virginia

Solid Ground Classic Reprints

First printing of new edition February 2007

Cover work by Borgo Design, Tuscaloosa, AL
Contact them at **borgogirl@bellsouth.net**

Cover image from Ric Ergenbright
View his work at ricergenbright.com

ISBN: 1-59925-096-9

TABLE OF CONTENTS

THE FIVE POINTS

OF

CALVINISM

HISTORICALLY, this title is of little accu-
racy or worth; I use it to denote certain
points of doctrine, because custom has made it
familiar. Early in the seventeenth century the
Presbyterian Church of Holland, whose doctrinal
Confession is the same in substance with ours,
was much troubled by a species of new-school
minority, headed by one of its preachers and pro-
fessors, James Harmensen, in Latin, *Arminius*
(hence, ever since, Arminians). Church and state
have always been united in Holland; hence the
civil government took up the quarrel. Professor
Harmensen *(Arminius)* and his party were re-
quired to appear before the State's General (what
we would call Federal Congress) and say what
their objections were against the doctrines of their
own church, which they had freely promised in their

ordination vows to teach. *Arminius* handed in a writing in which he named five points of doctrine concerning which he and his friends either differed or doubted. These points were virtually : Original sin, unconditional predestination, invincible grace in conversion, particular redemption, and perseverance of saints. I may add, the result was : that the Federal legislature ordered the holding of a general council of all the Presbyterian churches then in the world, to discuss anew and settle these five doctrines. This was the famous Synod of Dort, or Dordrecht, where not only Holland ministers, but delegates from the French, German, Swiss, and British churches met in 1618. The Synod adopted the rule that every doctrine should be decided by the sole authority of the word of God, leaving out all human philosophies and opinions on both sides. The result was a short set of articles which were made a part thenceforward of the Confession of Faith of the Holland Presbyterian Church. They are clear, sound, and moderate, exactly the same in substance with those of our Westminister Confession, enacted twenty-seven years afterward.

I have always considered this paper handed in by *Arminius* as of little worth or importance. It is neither honest nor clear. On several points

it seeks cunningly to insinuate doubts or to con-
fuse the minds of opponents by using the language
of pretended orthodoxy. But as the debate went
on, the differences of the Arminians disclosed
themselves as being, under a pretended new name,
nothing in the world but the old semi-pelagianism
which had been plaguing the churches for a
thousand years, the cousin-german of the Socin-
ian or Unitarian creed. Virtually it denied that
the fallen Adam had brought man's heart into
an entire and decisive alienation from God; it
asserted that his election of grace was not sovereign, but founded in his own foresight of the
faith, repentance and perseverance of such as
would choose to embrace the gospel. That grace
in effectual calling is not efficacious and invincible, but resistible, so that all actual conversions
are the joint result of this grace and the sinner's
will working abreast. That Christ died equally
for the non-elect and the elect, providing an indefinite, universal atonement for all; and that true
converts may, and sometimes do, fall away totally
and finally from the state of grace and salvation;
their perseverance therein depending not on efficacious grace, but on their own free will to continue
in gospel duties.

Let any plain mind review these five changes

and perversions of Bible truth, and he will see two facts: One, that the debate about them all will hinge mainly upon the first question, whether man's original sin is or is not a complete and decisive enmity to godliness; and the other, that this whole plan is a contrivance to gratify human pride and self-righteousness and to escape that great humbling fact everywhere so prominent in the real gospel, that man's ruin of himself by sin is utter, and the whole credit of his redemption from it is God's.

We Presbyterians care very little about the name Calvinism. We are not ashamed of it; but we are not bound to it. Some opponents seem to harbor the ridiculous notion that this set of doctrines was the new invention of the Frenchman John Calvin. They would represent us as in this thing followers of him instead of followers of the Bible. This is a stupid historical error. John Calvin no more invented these doctrines than he invented this world which God had created six thousand years before. We believe that he was a very gifted, learned, and, in the main, godly man, who still had his faults. He found substantially this system of doctrines just where we find them, in the faithful study of the Bible, where we see them taught by all the prophets, apostles, and the Messiah himself, from Genesis to Revelation.

Calvin also found the same doctrines handed down by the best, most learned, most godly, uninspired church fathers, as Augustine and Saint Thomas Aquinas, still running through the errors of popery. He wielded a wide influence over the Protestant churches; but the Westminster Assembly and the Presbyterian churches by no means adopted all Calvin's opinions. Like the Synod of Dort, we draw our doctrines, not from any mortal man or human philosophy, but from the Holy Ghost speaking in the Bible. Yet, we do find some inferior comfort in discovering these same doctrines of grace in the most learned and pious of all churches and ages ; of the great fathers of Romanism, of Martin Luther, of Blaise Paschal, of the original Protestant churches, German, Swiss, French, Holland, English and Scotch, and far the largest part of the real scriptural churches of our own day. The object of this tractate is simply to enable all honest inquirers after truth to understand just what those doctrines really are which people style the peculiar "doctrines of Presbyterians," and thus to enable honest minds to answer all objections and perversions. I do not write because of any lack in our church of existing treatises well adapted to our purpose; nor because I think anyone can now add anything really new to the argument. But our pastors and missionaries think that some additional good may come from another short discussion suitable for unprofessional readers. To such I would earnestly recommend two little books, Dr. Mathews's on the *Divine Purpose*, and Dr. Nathan Rice's *God Sovereign and Man Free*. For those who wish to investigate these doctrines more extensively there are, in addition to their Bible, the standard works in the English language on doctrinal divinity, such as *Calvin's Institutes* (translated), *Witsius on the Covenants*, Dr. William Cunningham's, of Edinburgh, Hill's and Dicks's *Theologies*, and in the United States those of Hodge, Dabney, and Shedd. All these can be purchased from or through our Assembly's Committee of Publication, No. 1001 Main street. Richmond, Va., and sent by mail.

I. What Presbyterians really mean by "Original Sin," "Total Depravity," and "Inability of Will"

Confession of Faith, Chapter IX., Section iii. "Man, by his fall into a state of sin, hath wholly lost all ability of will to any spiritual good accompanying salvation; so as a natural man being altogether averse from that good, and dead in sin, is not able, by his own strength, to convert himself, or to prepare himself thereunto."

By original sin we mean the evil quality which characterizes man's natural disposition and will. We call this sin of nature original, because each fallen man is born with it, and because it is the source or origin in each man of his actual transgressions.

By calling it total, we do not mean that men are from their youth as bad as they can be. Evil men and seducers wax worse and worse, " deceiving and being deceived." (2 Tim. iii. 13.) Nor do we mean that they have no social virtues towards their fellowmen in which they are sincere. We do not assert with extremists that because they are natural men, therefore all their friendship, honesty, truth, sympathy, patriotism, domestic love, are pretences or hypocrisies. What our Confession says is, " That they have wholly lost ability of will to any *spiritual good accompanying salvation*." The worst retain some, and the better much, ability of will for sundry moral goods accompanying social life. Christ teaches this (Mark x. 21) when, beholding the social virtues of the rich young man who came kneeling unto him, " *He loved him*," for Christ could never love mere hypocrisies.   What we teach is, that by the fall man's moral nature has undergone an utter change to sin, irreparable by himself. In this sense it is complete, decisive, or total. The state is as truly sinful as their actual transgressions, because it is as truly free and spontaneous.   This original sin shows itself in all natural men in a fixed and utter opposition of heart to some forms of duty, and especially and always to spiritual duties, owing to God, and in a fixed and absolutely decisive purpose of heart to continue in some sins (even while practicing some social duties), and especially to continue in their sins of unbelief, impenitence, self-will, and practical godlessness.   In this the most moral are as inflexibly determined by nature as the most immoral.   The better part may sincerely respect sundry rights and duties regarding their fellowmen, but in the resolve that self-will shall be their rule, whenever they please, as against God's sovereign holy will, these are as inexorable as the most wicked.   I suppose that a refined and genteelly reared young lady presents the least sinful specimen of unregenerate human nature.   Examine such a one.   Before she would be guilty of theft, profane swearing, drunkenness, or impurity, she would die.   In her opposition to these sins she is truly sincere. But there are some forms of self-will, especially in sins of omission as against God, in which she is just as determined as the most brutal drunkard is in his sensuality. She has, we will suppose, a Christian mother. She is determined to pursue certain fashionable conformities and dissipations. She has a light novel under her pillow which she intends to read on the Sabbath. Though she may still sometimes repeat like a parrot her nursery prayers, her's is spiritually a prayerless life. Especially is her heart fully set in her not to forsake at this time her life of self-will and worldliness for Christ's service and her salvation. Tenderly and solemnly her Christian mother may ask her, "My daughter, do you not know that in these things you are wrong toward your heavenly Father?" She is silent. She knows she is wrong. "My daughter, will you not therefore now relent, and choose for your Saviour's sake, this very day, the life of faith and repentance, and especially begin to-night the life of regular, real, secret prayer. Will you?" Probably her answer is in a tone of cold and bitter pain. "Mother, don't press me, I would rather not promise." No; *she will not!* Her refusal may be civil in form, because she is well-bred; but her heart is as inflexibly set in her as the hardened steel not at this time to turn truly from her self-will to her God.   In that particular her stubbornness is just the same as that of the most hardened sinners.   Such is the best type of unregenerate humanity.

Now, the soul's duties towards God are the highest, clearest, and most urgent of all duties; so that wilful disobedience herein is the most express, most guilty, and most hardening of all the sins that the soul commits.   God's perfections and will are the most supreme and perfect standard of moral right and truth.   Therefore, he who sets himself obstinately against God's right is putting himself in the most fatal and deadly opposition to moral goodness.   God's grace is the one fountain of holiness for rational creatures; hence, he who separates himself from this God by this hostile self-will, shuts himself in to ultimate spiritual death.   This rooted, godless, self-will is the eating cancer of the soul.   That soul may remain for a time like the body of a young person tainted with undeveloped cancer, apparently attractive and pretty.   But the cancer is spreading the secret seeds of corruption through all the veins; it will break out at last in putrid ulcers, the blooming body will become a ghastly corpse.   There is no human remedy.   To drop the figure; when the sinful soul passes beyond the social restraints and natural affections of this life, and beyond hope, into the world of the lost, this fatal root, sin of wilful godlessness will soon develop into all forms of malignity and wickedness; the soul will become finally and utterly dead to God and to good. This is what we mean by total depravity.

Once more, Presbyterians do not believe that men lose their *free-agency* because of original sin. See our Confession, Chapter IX., Section i.: "God hath endued the will of man with that natural liberty, that it is neither forced, nor by any absolute necessity of nature determined, to good or evil." We fully admit that where an agent is not free he is not morally responsible. A just God will never punish him for actions in which he is merely an instrument, impelled by the compulsion of external force or fate. But what is free-agency? There is no need to call in any abstruse metaphysics to the sufficient answer. Let every man's consciousness and common sense tell him: I know that I am free *whenever what I choose to do is the result of my own preference.*

I choose and act so as to please myself, then I am free. That is to say, our responsible volitions are the expression and the result of our own

rational preference. When I am free and responsible it is because I choose and do the thing
which I do, *not compelled by* some other agents,
but in accordance with my own inward preference. We all know self-evidently that this is so.
But is rational preference in us a mere haphazard
state? Do our reasonable souls contain no original principles regulative of their preferences and
choices? Were this so, then would man's soul be
indeed a miserable weathercock, wheeled about by
every outward wind; not fit to be either free,
rational or responsible. We all know that we
have such first principles regulative of our preferences: and these *are our own natural dispositions.*
They are inward, not external They are spontaneous, not compelled, and so as free as our
choices. They are our own, not somebody else's.
They are ourselves. They are essential attributes
in any being possessed of personality. Every
rational person must have some kind of natural
disposition. We can conceive of one person as
naturally disposed this way, and of another that
way. It is impossible for us to think a rational
free agent not disposed any way at all. Try it.
We have capital illustrations of what native disposition is in the corporeal propensities of ani.
mals. It is the nature of a colt to like grass and

hay. It is the nature of a bouncing schoolboy to like hot sausage. You may tole the colt with a bunch of nice hay, but not the boy; it is the hot sausage will fetch him when he is hungry; offer the hot sausage to the colt and he will reject it and shudder at it. Now both the colt and the boy *are free* in choosing what they like; free because their choices follow their own natural likings, *i. e.*, their own animal dispositions.

But rational man has mental dispositions which are better than illustrations, actual cases of native principles regulating natural choices. Thus, when happiness or misery may be chosen simply for their own sakes, every man's natural disposition is towards happiness and against misery. Again, man naturally loves property; all are naturally disposed to gain and to keep their own rather than to lose it for nothing. Once more, every man is naturally disposed to enjoy the approbation and praise of his fellow-men; and their contempt and abuse are naturally painful to him. In all these cases men choose according as they prefer, and they prefer according to their natural dispositions, happiness rather than misery, gain rather than loss, applause rather than abuse. They are as free in these choices as they are sure to choose in the given way. And they are as certain to choose agreeably to these original dispositions as rivers are to run downwards; equally certain and equally free, because the dispositions which certainly regulate their preferences are their own, not some one else's, and are spontaneous in them, not compelled.

Let us apply one of these cases. I make this appeal to a company of aspiring young ladies and gentlemen: "Come and engage with me of your free choice in this given course of labor; it will be long and arduous; but I can assure you of a certain result. I promise you that, by this laborious effort, you shall make yourselves the most despised and abused set of young people in the State. Will this succeed in inducing them? Can it succeed? No; it will not, and we justly say, it cannot. But are not these young persons free when they answer me, as they certainly will, " No, Teacher, we will not, and we cannot commit the folly of working hard solely to earn contempt, because contempt is in itself contrary and painful to our nature." This is precisely parallel to what Presbyterians mean by inability of will to all spiritual good. It is just as real and certain as inability of faculty. These people have the fingers wherewith to perform the proposed labor, let us say of writing, by which I invite them to toil for the earning of contempt. They have eyes and fingers wherewith to do penmanship, but they *cannot* freely choose my offer, because it contradicts that principle of their nature, love of applause, which infallibly regulates free, human preference and choice. Here is an exact case of "inability of will." If, now, man's fall has brought into his nature a similar native principle or disposition against godliness for its own sake, and in favor of self-will as against God, then a parallel case of inability of will presents itself. The former case explains the latter. The natural man's choice in preferring his self-will to God's authority is equally free, and equally certain. But this total lack of ability of will toward God does not suspend man's responsibility, because it is the result of his own free disposition, not from any compulsion from without. If a master would require his servant to do a bodily act for which he naturally had not the bodily faculty, as, for instance, the pulling up of a healthy oak tree with his hands, it would be unjust to punish the servant's failure. But this is wholly another case than the sinner's. For, if his natural disposition towards God were what it ought to be, he would not find himself deprived of the natural faculties by which God is known, loved, and served. The sinner's case is not one of extinction of faculties, but of their thorough wilful perversion. It is just like the case of Joseph's wicked brethren, of whom Moses says (Gen. xxxvii. 4): "That they hated their brother Joseph, so that they could not speak peaceably unto him." They had tongues in their heads? Yes. They could speak in words whatever they chose, but hatred, the wicked voluntary principle, ensured that they would not, and could not, speak kindly to their innocent brother.

Now, then, all the argument turns upon the question of fact: is it so that since Adam's fall the natural disposition of all men is in this state of fixed, decisive enmity against God's will, and fixed, inexorable preference for their own self-will, as against God? Is it true that man is in this lamentable state; that while still capable of being rightly disposed toward sundry virtues and duties, terminating on his fellow-creatures, his heart is inexorably indisposed and wilfully opposed to those duties which he owes to his heavenly Father directly? That is the question! Its best and shortest proof would be the direct appeal to every man's conscience. I know that it was just so with me for seventeen years, until God's almighty hand took away the heart of stone and gave me a heart of flesh. Every converted man confesses the same of himself. Every unconverted man well knows that it is now true of himself, if he would allow his judgment and conscience to look honestly within.   Unbeliever, you may at times desire even earnestly the impunity, the safety from hell, and the other selfish advantages of the Christian life; but did you ever prefer and desire that life for its own sake? Did you ever see the moment when you really wished God to subjugate all your self-will to his holy will?   No!   That is the very thing which the secret disposition of your soul utterly resents and rejects.   The retention of that self-will is the very thing which you so obstinately prefer, that as long as you dare you mean to retain it and cherish it, even at the known risk of an unprepared death and a horrible perdition.   But I will add other proofs of this awful fact, and especially the express testimony of the Holy Spirit :

There is the universal fact that all men sin more or less, and do it wilfully.   In the lives of most unrenewed men, sin reigns prevalently.   The large majority are dishonest, unjust, selfish, cruel, as far as they dare to be, even to their fellow-creatures, not to say utterly godless to their heavenly Father.   The cases like that of the well-bred young lady, described above, are relatively few, fatally defective as they are. This dreadful reign of sin in this world continues in spite of great obstacles, such as God's judgments and threatenings, and laborious efforts to curb it in the way of governments, restrictive laws and penalties, schools, family discipline, and churches. This sinning of human beings begins more or less as soon as the child's faculties are so developed as to qualify him for sinning intentionally. "The wicked go astray as soon as they be born, speaking lies." Now, a uniform result must proceed from a regular prior cause—there must be original sin in man's nature.

Even the great rationalistic philosopher, Emmanual Kant, believed and taught this doctrine. His argument is, that when men act in the aggregate and in national masses, they show out their real native dispositions, because in these concurrent actions they are not restrained by public opinion and by human laws restricting individual actions, and they do not feel immediate personal responsibility for what they do. The actions of men in the aggregate, therefore, shows what man's heart really is. Now, then, what are the morals of the nations towards each other and towards God? Simply those of foxes, wolves, tigers, and atheists. What national senate really and humbly

tries to please and obey God in its treatment
of neighbor nations? What nation trusts its
safety simply to the justice of its neighbors?
Look at the great standing armies and fleets!
Though the nation may include many God-fear-
ing and righteous persons, when is that nation
ever seen to forego a profitable aggression upon
the weak, simply because it is unjust before God?
These questions are unanswerable.

In the third place, all natural men, the decent
and genteel just as much as the vile, show this
absolute opposition of heart to God's will, and
preference for self-will in some sinful acts and by
rejecting the gospel. This they do invariably,
knowingly, wilfully, and with utter obstinacy, until they are made willing in the day of God's
power. They know with perfect clearness that
the gospel requirements of faith, trust, repentance,
endeavors after sincere obedience, God's righteous law, prayer, praise, and love to him, are reasonable and right. Outward objects or inducements are constantly presented to their souls,
which are of infinite moment, and ought to be
absolutely omnipotent over right hearts. These
objects include the unspeakable love of God in
Christ in giving his son to die for his ennmies,
which ought to melt the heart to gratitude in an

instant; the inexpressible advantages and blessings of an immortal heaven, secured by immediate faith, and the unutterable, infinite horrors of an everlasting hell, incurred by final unbelief, and risked to an awful degree, even by temporary hesitation. And these latter considerations appeal not only to moral conscience, but to that natural selfishness which remains in full force in unbelievers. Nor could doubts concerning these gospel truths, even if sincere and reasonably grounded to some extent, explain or excuse this neglect. For faith, and obedience, and the worship and the love of God, are self-evidently right and good for men, whether these awful gospel facts be true or not. He who believes is acting on the safe side in that he loses nothing, but gains something whichever way the event may go; whereas neglect of the gospel will have incurred an infinite mischief, with no possible gain should Christianity turn out to be true.

In such cases reasonable men always act, as they are morally bound to do, upon the safe side, under the guidance of even a slight probability. Why do not doubting men act thus on the safe side, even if it were a doubtful case (which it is not)? Because their dispositions are absolutely fixed and determined against godliness. Now,

what result do we see from the constant application of these immense persuasives to the hearts of
natural men?   *They invariably put them off;*
sometimes at the cost of temporary uneasiness or
agitation, but they infallibly put them off, prefer-
ing, as long as they dare, to gratify self-will at the
known risk of plain duty and infinite blessedness.
Usually they make this ghastly suicidal and
wicked choice with complete coolness, quickness,
and ease!   They attempt to cover from their
own consciences the folly and wickedness of
their decision by the fact they can do it so coolly
and unfeelingly.   My common sense tells me
that this very circumstance is the most awful and
ghastly proof of the reality and power of original
sin in them.   If this had not blinded them, they
would be horrified at the very coolness with which
they can outrage themselves and their Saviour.
I see two men wilfully murder each his enemy.
One has given the fatal stab in great agitation,
after agonizing hesitations, followed by pungent
remorse.   He is not yet an adept in murder.   I
see the other man drive his knife into the breast
of his helpless victim promptly, cooly, calmly,
jesting while he does it, and then cheerfully eat
his food with his bloody knife.   This is no
longer a man, but a fiend.

But the great proof is the Scripture. The whole Bible, from Genesis to Revelation, asserts this original sin and decisive ungodliness of will of all fallen men. Gen. vi. 3: "My spirit shall not always strive with man, *for that he also is flesh* (carnally minded)." Again, chap. vi. 5 : " God saw that every imagination of the man's heart was only evil continually." After the terrors of the flood, God's verdict on the survivors was still the same. Chap. viii. 21 : "I will not again curse the ground any more for man's sake; for the imagination of man's heart is evil from his youth."

Job, probably the earliest sacred writer, asks, " Who can bring a clean thing out of an unclean? not one." (Chap. xiv. 4.) David says: " Behold I was shapen in iniquity, and in sin did my mother conceive me." (Ps. li. 5.) The prophet asks (Jer. xiii. 23), " Can the Ethiopian change his skin, or the leopard his spots? then may ye also do good that are accustomed to do evil." Jeremiah says, chap. xvii. 9 : " The heart is deceitful above all things, *and desperately* wicked." What does desperately mean ? In the New Testament Christ says (John iii. 4 and 5), " That which is born of the flesh is flesh;" and ." Except ye be born again ye cannot see the kingdom of God." The Pharisees' hearts (decent.

moral men) are like unto whited sepulchres, which appear beautifully outwardly, but within are *full* of dead men's bones *and all uncleanness.* Does Christ exaggerate, and slander decent people?

Peter tells us (Acts viii. 23) that the spurious believer is "in the gall of bitterness and the bond of iniquity." Paul (Romans viii. 7): "The carnal mind is enmity against God: for it is not subject to the law of God, "neither indeed can be," (inability of will). (Ephesians ii.): "All men are by nature children of wrath . . . . and dead in trespasses and sins." Are not these enough?

II. The nature and agency of the moral revolution, named effectual calling or regeneration. This change must be more than an outer reformation of conduct, an inward revolution of first principles which regulate conduct. It must go deeper than a change of purpose as to sin and godliness; it must be a reversal of the original dispositions which hitherto prompted the soul to choose sin and reject godliness. Nothing less grounds a true conversion. As the gluttonous child may be persuaded by the selfish fear of pain and death to forego the dainties he loves, and to swallow the nauseous drugs which his palate loathes, so the ungodly man may be induced by

his self-righteousness and selfish fear of hell to
forbear the sins he still loves, and submit to the
religious duties which his secret soul still detests.
But, as the one practice is no real cure of the
vice of gluttony in the child, so the other is no
real conversion to godliness in the sinner. The
child must not only forsake, but really dislike his
unhealthy dainties; not only submit to swallow,
but really love, the medicines naturally nauseous
to him. Selfish fear can do the former; nothing
but a physiological change of constitution can do
the latter. The natural man must not only submit from selfish fear to the godliness which he
detested, he must love it for its own sake, and
hate the sins naturally sweet to him. No change
can be permanent which does not go thus deep;
nothing less is true conversion. God's call to
the sinner is: "My son, give me *thine heart.*"
(Proverbs xxiii. 26.) God requireth truth in the
inward parts and in the hidden parts: "Thou
shalt make me to know wisdom." (Psalm li. 6.)
"Circumcise therefore the foreskin of your heart."
(Deut. x. 16.) But hear especially Christ: "Either
make the tree good, and his fruit good; or else
make the tree corrupt, and his fruit corrupt."
(Matt. xii. 33.) We call the inward revolution of
principles *regeneration;* the change of life which

immediately begins from the new principles *conversion*. Regeneration is a summary act, conversion a continuous process. Conversion begins in, and proceeds constantly out of, regeneration, as does the continuous growth of a plant out of the first sprouting or quickening of its dry seed. In conversion the renewed soul is an active agent: "God's people are willing in the day of his power." The converted man chooses and acts the new life of faith and obedience heartily and freely, as prompted by the Holy Ghost. In this sense, "He works out his own salvation." (Phil. ii. 12.) But manifestly in regeneration, in the initial revolution of disposition, the soul does not act, but is a thing acted on. In this first point there can be no coöperation of the man's will with the divine power. The agency is wholly God's, and not man's, even in part. The vital change must be affected by immediate direct divine power. God's touch here may be mysterious; but it must be real, for it is proved by the seen results. The work must be sovereign and supernatural. Sovereign in this sense, that there is no will concerned in its effectuation except God's, because the sinner's will goes against it as invariably, as freely, until it is renewed; supernatural, because there is nothing at all in sinful

human nature to begin it, man's whole natural
disposition being to prefer and remain in a godless state. As soon as this doctrine is stated, it
really proves itself. In our second section we
showed beyond dispute that man's natural disposition and will are enmity against God. Does
enmity ever *turn itself* into love? Can nature
act above nature? Can the stream raise itself to
a higher level than its own source? Nothing can
be plainer than this, that since the native disposition and will of man are wholly and decisively
against godliness, there is no source within the
man out of which the new godly will can come;
into the converted man it has come; then it must
have come from without, solely from the divine
will.

But men cheat themselves with the notion that
what they call free-will may choose to respond to
valid outward inducements placed before it, so
that gospel truth and rational free-will coöper-
ating with it may originate the great change instead of sovereign, efficacious divine grace. Now,
any plain mind, if it will think, can see that this
is delusive. Is any kind of an object actual inducement to any sort of agent? No, indeed. Is
fresh grass an inducement to a tiger? Is bloody
flesh an inducement to a lamb to eat? Is a

nauseous drug an inducement to a child's palate;
or ripe sweet fruit?   Is useless loss an inducement to the merchant; or useful gain?   Are contempt and reproach inducements to aspiring
youth; or honor and fame ?   Manifestly some kinds
of objects only are inducements to given sorts of
agents; and the opposite objects are repellants.
Such is the answer of common sense.   Now, what
has decided which class of objects shall attract,
and which shall repel?   Obviously it is the agents'
own original, subjective dispositions which have
determined this.   It is the lamb's nature which
has determined that the fresh grass, and not the
bloody flesh, shall be the attraction to it.   It is
human nature in the soul which has determined
that useful gain, and not useless loss, shall be inducement to the merchant.   Now, then, to influence a man by inducement you must select an
object which his own natural disposition has
made attractive to him; by pressing the opposite
objects on him you only repel him; and the presentation of the objects can never reverse the
man's natural disposition, because this has determined in advance which objects will be attractions and which repellants.   Effects cannot reverse
the very causes on which they themselves depend.
The complexion of the child cannot re-determine

the complexion of the father. Now, facts and Scripture teach us (see 2d. Section) that man's original disposition is as freely, as entirely, against God's will and godliness and in favor of self-will and sin. Therefore, godliness can never be of itself inducement, but only repulsion, to the un-regenerate soul. Men cheat themselves; they think they are induced by the selfish advantages of· an imaginary heaven, an imaginary selfish escape from hell. But this is not regeneration; it is but the sorrows of the world that worketh death, and the hope of the hypocrite that per-isheth.

The different effects of the same preached gospel at the same time and place prove that re-generation is from sovereign grace : " Some be-lieved the things which were spoken, and some be-lieved not." (Acts xxviii. 24.) This is because, "As many as were ordained to eternal life believed." (Acts xiii. 48.) Often those remain unchanged whose social virtues, good habits, and amiability should seem to offer least obstruction to the gospel; while some old, profane, sensual, and hardened sinners become truly converted, whose wickedness and long confirmed habits of sinning must have presented the greatest obstruction· to gospel truth. Like causes ·should produce like effects. Had outward gospel inducements been the real causes, these results of preaching would be impossible. The facts show that the gospel inducements were only instruments, and that in the real conversions the agency was almighty grace.

The erroneous theory of conversion is again powerfully refuted by those cases, often seen, in which gospel truth has remained powerless over certain men for ten, twenty, or fifty years, and at last has seemed to prevail for their genuine conversion. The gospel, urged by the tender lips of a mother, proved too weak to overcome the self-will of the boy's heart. Fifty years afterwards that same gospel seemed to convert a hardened old man! There are two well-known laws of the human soul which show this to be impossible. One is, that facts and inducements often, but fruitlessly, presented to the soul, become weak and trite from vain repetition The other is, that men's active appetences grow stronger continually by their own indulgence. Here, then, is the case: The gospel when presented to the sensitive boy must have had much more force than it could have to the old man after it had grown stale to him by fifty years of vain repetition. The old man's love of sin must have grown greatly stronger than

the boy's by fifty years of constant indulgence.
Now how comes it, that a given moral influence
which was too weak to overcome the boy's sinful-
ness has overcome the old man's carnality when
the influences had become so much weaker and
the resistance to it so much stronger. This is
impossible. It was the finger of God, and not
the mere moral influence, which wrought the
mighty change. Let us suppose that fifty years
ago the reader had seen me visit his rural sanc-
tuary, when the grand oaks which now shade it
were but lithe saplings. He saw me make an
effort to tear one of them with my hands from its
seat; but it proved too strong for me. Fifty
years after, he and I meet at the same sacred
spot, and he sees me repeat my attempt upon the
same tree, now grown to be a monarch of the
grove. He will incline to laugh me to scorn:
"He attempted that same tree fifty years ago,
when he was in his youthful prime and it was but
a sapling, but he could not move it. Does the
old fool think to rend it from its seat now when
age has so diminished his muscle, and the sapling has grown to a mighty tree?" But let us
suppose that the reader saw that giant of the
grove come up in my aged hands. He would no
longer laugh. He would stand awe-struck. He

would conclude that this must be the hand of God, not of man. How vain is it to seek to break the force of this demonstration by saying that at last the moral influence of the gospel had received sufficient accession from attendant circumstances, from clearness and eloquence of presentation, to enable it to do its work? What later eloquence of the pulpit can rival that of the Christian mother presenting the cross in the tender accents of love. Again, the story of the cross, the attractions of heaven, ought to be immense, even when stated in the simplest words of childhood. How trivial and paltry are any additions which mere human rhetoric can make to what ought to be the infinite force of the naked truth.

But the surest proof is that of Scripture. This everywhere asserts that the sinner's regeneration is by sovereign, almighty grace. One class of texts presents those which describe the sinner's prior condition as one of "blindness," Eph. iv. 18 ; "of stony heartedness," Ezek. xxxvi. 26; "of impotency," Rom. v. 6 ; "of enmity," Rom. vii. 7 ; "of inability, John vi. 44, and Rom. vii. 18; "of deadness," Eph. ii. 1–5. Let no one exclaim that these are "figures of speech." Surely the Holy Spirit, when resorting to figures for the very purpose of giving a more forcible expression to truth, does not resort to a deceitful rhetoric! Surely he selects his figures because of the correct parallel between them and his truth!

Now, then, the blind man cannot take part in the very operation which is to open his eyes. The hard stone cannot be a source of softness. The helpless paralytic cannot begin his own restoration. Enmity against God cannot choose love for him. The dead corpse of Lazarus could have no agency in recalling the vital spirit into itself. After Christ's almighty power restored it, the living man could respond to the Saviour's command and rise and come forth.

The figures which describe the almighty change prove the same truth. It is described (Ps. cxix. 18) as an opening of the blind eyes to the law; as a new creation; (Ps. li. 10; Eph. ii. 5) as a new birth; (John iii. 3) as a quickening or resurrection (making alive); Eph. i. 18, and ii. 10). The man blind of cataract does not join the surgeon in couching his own eye; nor does the sunbeam begin and perform the surgical operation; that must take place in order for the light to enter and produce vision.

The timber is shaped by the carpenter; it does not shape itself, and does not become an implement until he gives it the desired shape.

The infant does not procreate itself, but must be born of its parents in order to become a living agent.

The corpse does not restore life to itself; after life is restored it becomes a living agent.

Express scriptures teach the same doctrine. In Jer. xxxi. 18, Ephraim is heard praying thus: " *Turn thou* me and I shall *be turned*." In John i. 12, we are taught that believers are born "not of blood, nor of the will of man, nor of the will of the flesh, but of God." In John vi. 44, Christ assures us that "No man can come to me except the Father which hath sent me draw him." And in chap. xv. 16, " Ye have not chosen me, but I have chosen you, and ordained you, that you should go and bring forth fruit." In Eph. ii. 10, "For we are his workmanship, created in Christ Jesus unto good works, which Christ hath fore-ordained that we should walk in them."

It is objected that this doctrine of almighty grace would destroy man's free-agency. This is not true. All men whom God does not regenerate retain their natural freedom unimpaired by anything which he does to them.

It is true that these use their freedom, as invariably, as voluntarily, by choosing their self-will and unregenerate state. But in doing this they

choose in perfect accordance with their own preference, and this the only kind of free-agency
known to men of common sense. The unregenerate choose just what they prefer, and therefore choose freely; but so long as not renewed
by almighty grace, they always prefer to remain
unregenerate, because it is fallen man's nature.
The truly regenerate do not lose their free-agency
by effectual calling, but regain a truer and higher
freedom; for the almighty power which renews
them does not force them into a new line of conduct contrary to their own preferences, but re-
verses the original disposition itself which regulates preference. Under this renewed disposition
they now act just as freely as when they were
voluntary sinners, but far more reasonably and
happily. For they act the new and right preference, which almighty grace has put in place of
the old one.

It is objected, again, that unless the agent has
exercised his free-will in the very first choice or
adoption of the new moral state, there could be
no moral quality and no credit for the series of
actions proceeding therefrom, because they would
not be voluntary. This is expressly false. True,
the new-born sinner can claim no merit for that
sovereign change of will in which his conversion

began, because it was not his own choosing, or doing, but God's; yet the cavil is untrue; the moral quality and merit of a series of actions does not depend on the question, whether the agent put himself into the moral state whence they flow, by a previous volition of his own starting from a moral indifference.

The only question is, whether his actions are sincere, and the free expressions of a right disposition, for

1. Then Adam could have no morality; for we are expressly told that God "created him upright." (Eccles. vii. 29.)

2. Jesus could have had no meritorious morality, because being conceived of the Holy Ghost he was born that holy thing. (Matt. i. 20; Luke i. 35.)

3. God himself could have no meritorious holiness, because he was and is eternally and unchangeably holy. He never chose himself into a state of holiness, being eternally and necessarily holy. Here, then, this miserable objection runs into actual blasphemy. On this point John Wesley is as expressly with us as Jonathan Edwards. See Wesley, *On Original Sin.*

III.

God's Election.

In our Confession, Chapter III., Section iii., verses 4 and 7, we have this description of it: 3d. "By the decree of God, for the manifestation of his glory, some men and angels are predestined unto everlasting life and others foreordained to everlasting death." IV. "These angels and men, thus predestinated and foreordained, are particularly and unchangeably designed; and their number is so certain and definite that it cannot be either increased or diminished."

VII. "The rest of mankind, God was pleased, according to the unsearchable counsel of his own will, whereby he extendeth or withholdeth mercy as he pleaseth, for the glory of his sovereign power over his creatures, to pass by and to ordain them to dishonor and wrath for their sin, to the praise of his glorious justice."

The first and second sections of this tract prove absolutely this sad but stubborn fact, that no sinner ever truly regenerates himself. One sufficient reason is, that none ever wish to do it, but always prefer, while left to themselves by God, to remain as they are, self-willed and worldly. That is to say, no sinner ever makes himself choose God and holiness, because every princi-

ple of his soul goes infallibly to decide the opposite preference. Therefore, whenever a sinner is
truly regenerated, *it must be God that has done
it.* Take notice, after God has done it, this
new-born sinner will, in his subsequent course of
repentance and conversion, freely put forth many
choices for God and holiness; but it is impossible
that this sinner can have put forth the first choice
to reverse his own natural principles of choice.
Can a child beget its own father? *It must have
been God that changed the sinner.* Then, when
he did it he meant to do it. *When was this intention to do it born into the divine mind?* That
same day? The day that sinner was born?
The day Adam was made? No! These answers
are all foolish. Because God is omniscient and
unchangeable he must have known from eternity
his own intention to do it. This suggests, second,
that no man can date any of God's purposes in time
without virtually denying his perfections of omniscience, wisdom, omnipotence, and immutability.
Being omniscient, it is impossible he should ever
find out afterwards anything he did not know
from the first. Being all-wise, it is impossible he
should take up a purpose for which his knowledge does not see a reason. Being all-powerful,
it is impossible he should ever fail in trying to

effect one of his purposes. Hence, whatever
God does in nature or grace, he intended to do
that thing from eternity. Being unchangeable, it
is impossible that he should change his mind to a
different purpose after he had once made it up
aright under the guidance of infinite knowledge,
wisdom, and holiness. All the inferior wisdom of
good men but illustrates this. Here is a wise
and righteous general conducting a defensive
war to save his country. At mid-summer an observer says to him, "General, have you not
changed your plan of campaign since you began
it?" He replies, "I have." Says the observer,
"Then you must be a fickle person?" He replies, "No, I have changed it not because I was
fickle, but for these two reasons : because I have
been unable and have failed in some of the
necessary points of my first plan; and second, I
have found out things I did not know when I
began." We say that is perfect common sense,
and clears the general from all charge of fickleness. But suppose he were, in fact, almighty and
omniscient? Then he could not use those ex-
cuses, and if he changed his plan after the beginning he would be fickle. Reader, dare you
charge God with fickleness? This is a sublime
conception of God's nature and actions, as far

above the wisest man's as the heavens above the earth. But it is the one taught us everywhere in Scripture. Let us beware how in our pride of self-will we blaspheme God by denying it. *Third.* Arminians themselves virtually admit the force of these views and scriptures; for their doctrinal books expressly admit God's particular personal election of every sinner that reaches heaven. A great many ignorant persons suppose that the Arminian theology denies all particular election. This is a stupid mistake. Nobody can deny it without attacking the Scripture, God's perfections, and common sense. The whole difference between Presbyterians and intelligent Arminians is this: We believe that God's election of individuals is unconditioned and sovereign. *They believe that while eternal and particular, it is on account of God's eternal, omniscient foresight of the given sinner's future faith, repentance, and perseverance in holy living.* But we Presbyterians must dissent for these reasons: It is inconsistent with the eternity, omnipotence, and sovereignty of the great *first cause* to represent his eternal purposes thus, as grounded in, or conditioned on, anything which one of his dependent creatures would hereafter contingently do or leave undone.

Will or will not that creature ever exist in the future to do or to leave undone any particular thing? That itself must depend on God's sovereign creative power. We must not make an independent God depend upon his own dependent creature. But does not Scripture often represent a salvation or ruin of sinners as conditioned on their own faith or unbelief? Yes. But do not confound two different things. The result ordained by God may depend for its rise upon the suitable means. But the acts of God's mind in ordaining it does not depend on these means, because God's very purpose is this, to bring about the means without fail and the result by the means.

Next, whether God's election of a given sinner, say, Saul of Tarsus, be conditioned or not upon the foresight of his faith, if it is an eternal and omniscient foresight *it must be a certain one.* Common sense says: no cause, no effect; an uncertain cause can only give an uncertain effect. Says the Arminian : God certainly foresaw that Saul of Tarsus would believe and repent, and, therefore, elected him. But I say, that if God certainly foresaw Saul's faith, it must have been certain to take place, for the Omniscient cannot make mistakes. Then, if this sinner's faith was certain to take place, there must have been some certain cause insuring that it would take place. Now, no certain cause could be in the "free-will" of this sinner, Saul, even as aided by "common sufficient grace." For Arminians say, that this makes and leaves the sinner's will contingent. Then, whatever made God think that this sinner, Saul, would ever be certain to believe and repent? Nothing but God's own sovereign eternal will to renew him unto faith and repentance.

This leads to the crowning argument. This Saul was by nature "dead in trespasses and in sins" (Eph. ii. 1), and, therefore, would never have in him any faith or repentance to be fore-seen, except as the result of God's purpose to put them in him. But the effect cannot be the cause of its own cause. The cart cannot pull the horse; why, it is the horse that pulls the cart. This is expressly confirmed by Scripture. Christ says (John xv. 16): "Ye have not chosen me, but I have chosen you, and ordained you, that ye should go and bring forth fruit, and that your fruit should remain." Romans ix. 11–13: "For the children being not yet born, neither having done any good or evil, that the purpose of God according to election might stand, not of works, but of him that calleth; It was said unto her, The elder shall serve the younger. As it is written, Jacob have I loved, but Esau have I hated;" and verse 16: "So then, it is not of him that willeth, nor of him that runneth, but of God that sheweth mercy." What is not? The connection shows that it is the election of the man that willeth and runneth, of which the apostle here speaks. Paul here goes so dead against the notion of conditional election, that learned Arminians see that they must find some evasion, or squarely take the ground of infidels. This is their evasion: that by the names Esau and Jacob the individual patriarchs are not meant, but the two nations, Edom and Israel, and that the predestination was only unto the privation or enjoyment of the means of grace. But this is utterly futile: *First*, Because certainly the individual patriarchs went along with the two posterities whom they represented. *Second*, Because Paul's discussion in this ninth chapter all relates to individuals and not to races, and to salvation or perdition, and not to mere church privileges. *Third*, Because the preterition of the Edomite race from all gospel means must have resulted in the perdition of the individuals. For, says Paul: "How could they believe on him of whom they have not heard?"

This is the right place to notice the frequent

mistake when we say that God's election is sovereign and not conditioned on his foresight of the elected man's piety. Many pretend to think that we teach God has no reason at all for his choice; that we make it an instance of sovereign divine caprice! We teach no such thing. It would be impiety. Our God is too wise and righteous to have any caprices. He has a reasonable motive for every one of his purposes; and his omniscience shows him it is always the best reason. But he is not bound to publish it to us. God knew he had a reason for preferring the sinner, Jacob, to the sinner Esau. But this reason could not have been any forseeing merit of Jacob's piety by two arguments: The choice was made before the children were born. There never was any piety in Jacob to foresee, except what was to follow after as an effect of Jacob's election. Esau appears to have been an open, hard-mouthed, profane person. Jacob, by nature, a mean, sneaking hypocrite and supplanter. Probably God judged their personal merits as I do, that personally Jacob was a more detestable sinner than Esau. Therefore, on grounds of foreseen personal deserts, God could never have elected either of them. But his omniscience saw a separate, independent reason why it was wisest to make the worse man the object of his infinite mercy, while leaving the other to his own profane choice. Does the Arminian now say that I must tell him what that reason was? I answer, I do not know, God has not told me. But I know he had a good reason, because he is God. Will any man dare to say that because omniscience could not find its reason in the foreseen merits of Jacob, therefore it could find none at all in the whole infinite sweep of its providence and wisdom? This would be arrogance run mad and near to blasphemy.

One more argument for election remains: Many human beings have their salvation or ruin practically decided by providential events in their lives. The argument is, that since these events are sovereignly determined by God's providence, the election, or preterition of their souls is thereby virtually decided. Take two instances: Here is a wilful, impenitent man who is down with fever and is already delirious. Will he die or get well? God's providence will decide that. " In his hands our breath is, and his are all our ways." (Dan. v. 23.) If he dies this time he is too delirious to believe and repent; if he recovers, he may attend revival meetings and return to God. The other instance is, that of dying infants. This is peculiarly deadly to the Arminian theory, because they say so positively that all humans who die in infancy are saved. (And they slander us Presbyterians by charging that we are not positive enough on that point, and that we believe in the "damnation of infants.") Well, here is a human infant three months old. Will it die of croup, or will it live to be a man? God's providence will decide that. If it dies, the Arminian is certain its soul is gone to heaven, and therefore was elected of God to go there. If it is to grow to be a man, the Arminian says he may exercise his free-will to be a Korah, Dalthan, Abiram, or Judas. *But the election of the baby who dies cannot be grounded in God's foresight of its faith and repentance*, because there was none to foresee before it entered glory; the little soul having been redeemed by sovereign grace without these means.

But there is that sentence in our Confession, Chapter X., Section iii.: "Elect infants, dying in infancy, are regenerated and saved by Christ through the Spirit, who worketh when and where and how he pleaseth." Our charitable accusers will have it that the antithesis which we imply to the words "elect infants dying in infancy" is, that there are non-elect infants dying in infancy are so damned.   This we always deny.   But they seem to know what we think better than we know ourselves.   The implied antithesis we hold is this: There are elect infants not dying in infancy, and such must experience effectual calling through rational means, and freely believe and repent according to Chapter X.   There were once two Jewish babies, John and Judas; John an elect infant, Judas a non-elect one.   Had John the Baptist died of croup he would have been redeemed without personal faith and repentance; but he was predestinated to live to man's estate, so he had to be saved through effectual calling. Judas, being a non-elect infant, was also predestinated to live to manhood and receive his own fate freely by his own contumacy.   Presbyterians do not believe that the Bible or their Confession teaches that there are non-elect infants dying in infancy and so damned.   Had they thought this of their Confession, they would have changed this section long ago.

When an intelligent being makes a selection of some out of a number of objects, he therein unavoidably makes a preterition (a passing by) of the others; we cannot deny this without imputing ignorance or inattention to the agent; but omniscience can neither be ignorant nor inattentive.

Hence, God's preordination must extend to the saved and the lost.

But here we must understand the difference between God's effective decree and his permissive decree, the latter is just as definite and certain as the former; but the distinction is this: The objects of God's effective decree are effects which he himself works, without employing or including the free-agency of any other rational responsible person, such as his creations, miracles, regenerations of souls, resurrections of bodies, and all those results which his providence brings to pass, through the blind, compulsory powers of second causes, brutish or material. The nature of his purpose here is by his own power to determine these results to come to pass.

But the nature of his permissive decree is this: He resolves to allow or permit some creature free-agent freely and certainly to do the thing decreed without impulsion from God's power. To this class of actions belong all the indifferent, and especially all the sinful, deeds of natural men, and all those final results where such persons throw away their own salvation by their own disobedience. In all these results God does not himself do the thing, nor help to do it, but intentionally lets it be done. Does one ask how then

a permissive decree can have entire certainty?
The answer is, because God knows that men's
natural disposition certainly prompts them to evil;
for instance, I know it is the nature of lambs to
eat grass.   If I intentionally leave open the gate
between the fold and the pasture I know that the
grass will be eaten, and I intend to allow it just
as clearly as if I had myself driven them upon
the pasture.

Now, it is vain for those to object that God's
will cannot have anything to do with sinful results,
even in this permissive sense, without making
God an author of the sin, unless these cavillers
mean to take the square infidel ground.   For the
Bible is full of assertions that God does thus fore-
ordain sin without being an author of sin.   He
foreordained Pharaoh's tyranny and rebellion, and
then punished him for it.   In Isaiah x. he foreordains
Nebuchadnezzar's sack of Jerusalem, and then pun-
ishes him for it.   In Acts ii. 23 the wicked Judas
betrays his Lord by the determinate purpose and
foreknowledge of God.   In Romans ix. 18, "he
hath mercy on whom he will have mercy, and
whom he will he hardeneth," so in many other
places.   But our Confession, Chapter X., Section
vii., makes this express difference between God's
decree of election and of preterition.   The former

is purely gracious, not grounded in any foresight of any piety in them because they have none to foresee, except as they are elected and called, and in consequence thereof. But the non-elect are passed by and foreordained to destruction "*for their sins*, and for the glory of God's justice."

We thus see that usual fiery denunciations of this preterition are nothing but absurd follies and falsehoods. These vain-talkers rant as though it was God's foreordination which *makes these men go* to perdition. In this there is not one word of truth. They alone make themselves go, and God's purpose concerning the wretched result never goes a particle further than this, that in his justice he resolves to let them have their own preferred way. These men talk as though God's decree of preterition was represented by us as a barrier preventing poor striving sinners from getting to heaven, no matter how they repent and pray and obey, only because they are not the secret pets of an unjust divine caprice.

The utter folly and wickedness of this cavil are made plain by this, that the Bible everywhere teaches none but the elect and effectually called ever work or try in earnest to get to heaven; that the lost never really wish nor try to be saints; that their whole souls are opposed to it, and they prefer freely to remain ungodly, and this is the sole ·cause of their ruin. If they would truly repent, believe, and obey, they would find no decree debarring them from grace and heaven, God can say this just as the shepherd might say of the wolves: if they will choose to eat my grass peaceably with my lambs they shall find no fence of mine keeping them from my grass. But the shepherd knows that it is always the nature of wolves to choose to devour the lambs instead of the grass, which former their own natures, and not the fence, assuredly prompts them to do, until almighty power new-creates them into lambs. The reason why godless men cavil so fiercely against this part of the doctrine, and so foully misrepresent it, is just this : that they hate to acknowledge to themselves that free yet stubborn godlessness of soul which leads them voluntarily to work their own ruin, and so they try to throw the blame on God or his doctrine instead of taking it on themselves.

In fine, unbelieving men are ever striving to paint the doctrine of *election* as the harsh, the exclusive, the terrible doctrine, erecting a hindrance between sinners and salvation. But properly viewed it is exactly the opposite. It is not

the harsh doctrine, but the sweet one, not the
exclusive doctrine, not the hindrance of our salvation, but the blessed inlet to all the salvation
found in this universe. It is sin, man's voluntary
sin, which excludes him from salvation; and in
this sin God has no responsibility. It is God's
grace alone which persuades men both to come
in and remain within the region of salvation;
and all this grace is the fruit of election. I repeat, then, it is our voluntary sin which is the
source of all that is terrible in the fate of ruined
men and angels. It is God's election of grace
which is the sweet and blessed source of all that
is remedial, hopeful, and happy in earth and
heaven. God can say to every angel and redeemed man in the universe: "I have chosen
thee in everlasting love; therefore in loving kind-
ness have I drawn thee." And every angel and
saint on this earth and in glory responds, in accordance with our hymn:

> "Why was I made to hear his voice
>   And enter while there's room,
> While others make a wretched choice
>   And rather starve than come?
> 'Twas the same love that spread the **feast**
>   That sweetly drew me in;
> Else I had still refused to taste
>   And perish in my sin."

And now dare any sinner insolently press the question, why the same electing love and power in God did not also include and save all lost sinners? This is the sufficient and the awful answer: "Who art thou, O man, that repliest against God?" (Romans ix. 20.) Hast thou any claim of right against God, O man, to force thee against thy preference and stubborn choice to embrace a redemption unto holiness which thou dost hate and wilfully reject in all the secret powers of thy soul? And if thou destroyest thyself, while holy creatures may lament thy ruin, all will say that thou art the last being in this universe to complain of injustice, since this would be only complaining against the God whom thou dost daily insult, *that he did not make thee do the things and live the life which thou didst thyself wilfully and utterly refuse!*

Others urge this captious objection: that this doctrine of election places a fatal obstacle between the anxious sinner and saving faith. They ask, How can I exercise a sincere, appropriating faith, unless I have ascertained that I am elected? For the reprobate soul is not entitled to believe that Christ died for him, and as his salvation is impossible, the truest faith could not save him even if he felt it. But how can man as-

certain God's secret purpose of election toward
him?

This cavil expressly falsifies God's teachings
concerning salvation by faith. As concerning
his election the sinner is neither commanded
nor invited to embrace as the object of his
faith the proposition " I am elected." There
is no such command in the Bible. The proposition he is invited and commanded to embrace is this : "*Whosoever believeth* shall be
saved." (Rom. x. 11.) God has told this cavi-
ler expressly, "Secret things belong to the Lord
our God, but the things that are revealed belong
to you and your children, that ye may do all the
words of this law." (Deut. xxix. 29.) Let us
not cavil, but obey. God's promises also assure
us "that whosoever cometh unto God through
Christ, he will in no wise cast off." (John vi. 37.)
So that it is impossible that any sinner really
wishing to be saved can be kept from salvation
by uncertainty about his own election. When
we add that God's decree in no wise infringes
man's free agency, our answer is complete. Confession, Chapter III., Section i., by this decree,
" No violence is offered to the will of the creatures, nor is the liberty or contingency of second
causes taken away, but rather established."

But it is stubbornly objected that those who are subject to a sovereign, immutable decree cannot be free agents; that the two propositions are contradictory, and the assertion of both an insult to reason. We explained that there are various means by which we see free agents prompted to action, which are not compulsory, and yet certain of effect, and that our God is a God of infinite wisdom and resources. God tells them that in governing his rational creatures according to his eternal purpose, he uses only such means as are consistent with their freedom. Still, the arrogant objectors are positive that it cannot be done, even by an infinite God! that if there is predestination, there cannot be free-agency. Surely the man who makes this denial should be himself infinite!

But, perhaps, the best answer to this folly is this: Mr. Arminian, *you, a puny mortal, are actually doing, and that often, the very thing you say an almighty God cannot do! Predestinating the acts of free-agents, certainly and efficiently, without infringing their freedom.* For instance: Mr. Arminian invites me to dine with him at one o'clock P. M. I reply, yes, provided dinner is punctual and certain, because I have to take a railroad train at two P. M. He promises posi-

tively that dinner shall be ready at one P. M.
How so, will he cook it himself?   Oh, no ! but
he employs a steady cook, named Gretchen, and
he has already instructed her that one P. M.
must be the dinner hour.

That is predestination he tells me, certain and
efficacious.

I now take up Mr. Arminian's argument, and apply it to Gretchen thus :   He says predestination
and free-agency are contradictory.   He predestinated *you, Gretchen*, to prepare dinner for one
o'clock, therefore you were not a free agent in
getting dinner.   Moreover, as there can be no
moral desert where there is no freedom, you
have not deserved your promised wages for cook-
ing, and Mr. Arminian thinks he is not at all
bound to pay you.

Gretchen's common sense replies thus : *I know*
I *am* a free agent; I am no slave, no machine,
but a free woman, and an honest woman, who
got dinner at one o'clock because I chose to
keep my word; and if Mr. Arminian robs me of
my wages on this nasty pretext, I will know he is
a rogue.

Gretchen's logic is perfectly good.

My argument is, that men are perpetually predestinating and efficiently procuring free acts

of free agents.   How much more may an infinite God do likewise.   But this reasoning need not, and does not, imply that God's ways of doing it are the same as ours.

His resources of wisdom and power are manifold, infinite.   Thus this popular cavil is shown to be as silly and superficial as it is common.   It is men's sinful pride of will which makes them repeat such shallow stuff.

Having exploded objections, I now close this argument for election with the strongest of all the testimonies, *the Scriptures*.   The Bible is full of it; all of God's prophecies imply predestination, because, unless he had foreordained the predicted events, he could not be certain they would come to pass.   The Bible doctrine of God's providence proves predestination, because the Bible says providence extends to everything, and is certain and omnipotent, and it only executes what predestination plans.   Here are a few express texts among a hundred: Ps. xxxiii. 11 : "The counsel of the Lord standeth forever, the thoughts of his heart to all generations."   Is. xlvi. 10 : God declareth "the end from the beginning, and from ancient times the things that are not yet done, saying, my counsel shall stand, and I will do all my pleasure."   God's election of Israel was unconditional. See Ezek. xvi. 6 : "And when I passed by thee and saw thee polluted in thine own blood, I said unto thee when thou wast in thy blood, Live." Acts xiii. 48 : " When the Gentiles heard this . . . as many as were ordained to eternal life believed." Rom. viii. 29, 30 : "For whom he did foreknow, he also did predestinate. . . . Moreover, whom he did predestinate, them he also called, and whom he called, them he also justified; and whom he justified, them he also glorified." Eph. i. 4–7 : "He hath chosen us in him (Christ) before the foundation of the world," etc. 1 Thess. i. 4: "Knowing, brethren, beloved, your election of God." Rev. xxi. 27. " . . They that are written in the Lamb's book of life."

Silly people try to say that election is the doc-·trine of that harsh apostle Paul. But the loving Saviour teaches it more expressly if possible than Paul does. See, again, John xv. 16 : " Ye have not chosen me, but I have chosen you," etc. John vi. 37 : "All that the Father giveth me shall come to me," etc.; see also verses 39, 44 ; Matt. xxiv. 22 ; Luke xviii. 7 ; John x. 14, 28 ; Mark xiii. 22 ; Matt. xx. 16.

IV.

PARTICULAR REDEMPTION.

"Did Christ die for the elect only, or for all men?" The answer has been much prejudiced by ambiguous terms, such as "particular atonement," "limited atonement," or "general atonement," "unlimited atonement," "indefinite atonement." What do they mean by atonement? The word (at-one-ment) is used but once in the New Testament (Rom. v. 11), and there it means expressly and exactly *reconciliation*. This is proved thus: the same Greek word in the next verse, carrying the very same meaning, is translated reconciliation. Now, people continually mix two ideas when they say atonement: One is, that of the expiation for guilt provided in Christ's sacrifice. The other is, the individual reconciliation of a believer with his God, grounded on that sacrifice made by Christ once for all, but actually effectuated only when the sinner believes and by faith. The last is the true meaning of atonement, and in that sense every atonement (at-one-ment), reconciliation, must be individual, particular, and limited to this sinner who now believes. There have already been just as many atonements as there are true believers in heaven and earth, each one individual.

But sacrifice, expiation, is one—the single, glorious, indivisible act of the divine Redeemer, infinite and inexhaustible in merit. Had there been but one sinner, Seth, elected of God, this whole divine sacrifice would have been needed to expiate his guilt. Had every sinner of Adam's race been elected, the same one sacrifice would be sufficient for all. We must absolutely get rid of the mistake that expiation is an aggregate of gifts to be divided and distributed out, one piece to each receiver, like pieces of money out of a bag to a multitude of paupers. Were the crowd of paupers greater, the bottom of the bag would be reached before every pauper got his alms, and more money would have to be provided. I repeat, this notion is utterly false as applied to Christ's expiation, because it is a divine act. It is indivisible, inexhaustible, sufficient in itself to cover the guilt of all the sins that will ever be committed on earth. This is the blessed sense in which the Apostle John says (1st Epistle ii. 2): "Christ is the propitiation (the same word as ex. piation) for the sins of the whole world."

But the question will be pressed, "Is Christ's sacrifice limited by the purpose and design of the Trinity"? The best answer for Presbyterians to make is this: In the purpose and design of the

Godhead, *Christ's sacrifice was intended to effect just the results, and all the results, which would be found flowing from it in the history of redemption.*   I say this is exactly the answer for us Presbyterians to make, because we believe in God's universal predestination as certain and efficacious; so that the whole final outcome of his plan must be the exact interpretation of what his plan was at first.   *And this statement the Arminian also is bound to adopt, unless he means to charge God with ignorance, weakness, or fickleness.*   Search and see.

Well, then, the realized results of Christ's sacrifice are not one, but many and various :

1. It makes a display of God's general benevolence and pity towards all lost sinners, to the glory of his infinite grace.   For, blessed be his name, he says, " I have no pleasure in the death of him that dieth."

2. Christ's sacrifice has certainly purchased for the whole human race a merciful postponement of the doom incurred by our sins, including all the temporal blessings of our earthly life, all the gospel restraints upon human depravity, and the sincere offer of heaven to all.   For, but for Christ, man's doom would have followed instantly after his sin, as that of the fallen angels did.

3. Christ's sacrifice, wilfully rejected by men, sets the stubbornness, wickedness and guilt of their nature in a much stronger light, to the glory of God's final justice.

4. Christ's sacrifice has purchased and provided for the effectual calling of the elect, with all the graces which insure their faith, repentance, justification, perseverance, and glorification. *Now, since the sacrifice actually results in all these different consequences, they are all included in God's design.* This view satisfies all those texts quoted against us.

But we cannot admit that Christ died as fully and in the same sense for Judas as he did for Saul of Tarsus. Here we are bound to assert that, while the expiation is infinite, redemption is particular. The irrefragable grounds on which we prove that the redemption is particular are these : From the doctrines of unconditional election, and the covenant of grace. (The argument is one, for the covenant of grace is but one aspect of election.) The Scriptures tell us that those who are to be saved in Christ are a number definitely elected and given to him from eternity to be redeemed by his mediation. How can anything be plainer from this than that there was a purpose in God's expiation, as to them, other than that it

was as to the rest of mankind?   See Scriptures.
The immutability of God's purposes.   (Isa. xlvi.
10; 2 Tim. ii. 19.)   If God ever intended to save
any soul in Christ (and he has a definite intention
to save or not to save towards souls), that soul will
certainly be saved.   (John x. 27, 28; vi. 37–40.)
Hence, all whom God ever intended to save in
Christ will be saved.   But some souls will never
be saved; therefore some souls God never intended to be saved by Christ's atonement.   The
strength of this argument can scarcely be over-
rated.   Here it is seen that a limit as to the intention of the expiation must be asserted to rescue
God's power, purpose, and wisdom.   The same
fact is proved by this, that Christ's intercession is
limited.   (See John xvii. 9, 20.)   We know that
Christ's intercession is always prevalent.   (Rom.
viii. 34; John xi. 42.)   If he interceded for all,
all would be saved.   But all will not be saved.
Hence, there are some for whom he does not plead
the merit of his expiation.   But he is the "same
yesterday and to-day and forever."   Hence, there
were some for whom, when he made expiation,
he did not intend to plead it.   Some sinners (*i.
e.*, elect) receive from God gifts of conviction,
regeneration, faith, persuading and enabling them
to embrace Christ, and thus make his expiation

effectual to themselves, while other sinners do not. But these graces are a part of the purchased redemption, and bestowed through Christ. Hence his redemption was intended to effect some as it did not others. (See above.)

Experience proves the same. A large part of the human race were already in hell before the expiation was made. Another large part never hear of it. But "faith cometh by hearing" (Rom. x.), and faith is the condition of its application. Since their condition is determined intentionally by God's providence, it could not be his intention that the expiation should avail for them equally with those who hear and believe. This view is destructive, particularly of the Arminian scheme.

"Greater love hath no man than this, that a man lay down his life for his friends." But the greater includes the less, whence it follows, that if God the Father and Christ cherished for a given soul the definite electing love which was strong enough to pay the sacrifice of Calvary, it is not credible that this love would then refuse the less costly gifts of effectual calling and sustaining grace. This is the very argument of Rom. v. 10, and viii. 31–39. This inference would not be conclusive if drawn merely from the benevolence of God's nature, sometimes called in Scripture "his love", but in every case of his definite, electing love it is demonstrative.

Hence, it is absolutely impossible for us to retain the dogma that Christ in design died equally for all. We are compelled to hold that he died for Peter and Paul in some sense in which he did not for Judas. No consistent mind can hold the Calvinistic creed as to man's total depravity towards God, his inability of will, God's decree, God's immutable attributes of sovereignty and omnipotence over free agents, omniscience and wisdom, and stops short of this conclusion. So much every intelligent opponent admits, and in disputing particular redemption, to this extent at least, he always attacks these connected truths as falling along with the other.

In a word, Christ's work for the elect does not merely put them in a salvable state, but purchases for them a complete and assured salvation. To him who knows the depravity and bondage of his own heart, any less redemption than this would bring no comfort.

V.

PERSEVERANCE OF THE SAINTS.

Our Confession, in Chapter XVII., Sections i.

and ii., states this doctrine thus: "They whom God hath accepted in his beloved, effectually called and sanctified by his Spirit, can neither totally nor finally fall away from the state of grace, but shall certainly persevere therein to the end, and be eternally saved." "This perseverance of the saints depends not upon their own free will, but upon the immutability of the decree of election, flowing from the free and unchangeable love of God the Father; upon the efficacy of the merit and intercession of Jesus Christ; the abiding of the Spirit and of the seed of God within them; and the nature of the covenant of grace, from all which ariseth also the certainty and infallibility thereof."

I beg the reader to weigh these statements with candor and close attention. He will find that we do not ascribe this stability of grace in the believer to any excellence in his own soul, even regenerate, as source and cause, but we ascribe it to the unchangeable purpose and efficacious grace of God dwelling and operating in them. All the angels, and Adam, received from their Creator holy natures; yet our first father and the fallen angels show that they could totally fall away into sin. No one in himself is absolutely incapable of sinning, except the unchangeable

God.   Converted men, who still have indwelling sin, must certainly be as capable of falling as Adam, who had none.   We believe that the saints will certainly stand, because the God who chose them will certainly hold them up.

We do not believe that all professed believers and church members will certainly preserve and reach heaven.   It is to be feared that many such, even plausible pretenders, "have but a name to live while they are dead."   They fall fatally because they never had true grace to fall from.

We do not teach that any man is entitled to believe that he is justified, and therefore shall not come again in condemnation on the proposition "once in grace always in grace," although he be now living in intentional, wilful sin.   This falsehood of Satan we abhor.   We say, the fact that this deluded man can live in wilful sin is the strongest possible proof that he never was justified, and never had any grace to fall from.   And, once for all, no intelligent believer can possibly abuse this doctrine into a pretext for carnal security.   It promises to true believers a *perseverance in holiness*.   Who, except an idiot, could infer from that promise the privilege to be unholy?

Once more.   We do not teach that genuine believers are secure from backsliding, but if they

become unwatchful and prayerless, they may fall
for a time into temptations, sins, and loss of hope
and comfort, which may cause them much misery
and shame, and out of which a covenant-keeping
God will recover them by sharp chastisements
and deep contrition. Hence, so far as lawful
self-interests can be a proper motive for Christian
effort, this will operate on the Presbyterian under
this doctrinal perseverance, more than on the
Arminian with his doctrine of falling from grace.
The former cannot say, I need not be alarmed
though I be backslidden; for if he is a true believer he has to be brought back by grievous and
perhaps by terrible afflictions; he had better be
alarmed at these! But further, an enlightened
self-love will alarm him more pungently than the
Arminians' will him. Here is an Arminian who
finds himself backslidden. Does he feel a whole-
some alarm, saying to himself, "Ah, me, I was in
the right road to heaven, but I have gotten out of
it; I must get back into it." Well, the Presbyterian similarly backslidden is taught by his doctrine to say : *I thought* I was in the right road to
heaven, but now I see I was mistaken all the
time, because God says, that if I had really been
in that right road I could never have left it.
Alas! therefore, I must either perish or get back,

not to that old deceitful road in which I was, but into a new one, essentially different, narrower and straighter. Which of the two men has the more pungent motive to strive?

As I have taken the definition of the doctrine from our Confession, I will take thence the heads of its proofs:

(a), The immutability of God's election proves it. How came this given sinner to be now truly converted? Because God had elected him to salvation. But God says, "my purpose shall stand, and I will do all my pleasure." Since God is changeless and almighty, this purpose to save him must certainly succeed. But no man can be saved in his sins, therefore this man will certainly be made to persevere in grace.

(b), The doctrine follows from the fact that God's election is sovereign and unconditional, not grounded in any foreseen merit in the sinner elected. God knew there was none in him to foresee. But God did foresee all the disobedience, unthankfulness, and provocation which that unworthy sinner was ever to perpetrate. Therefore, the future disclosure of this unthankfulness, disobedience, and provocation by this poor sinner, cannot become a motive with God to revoke his election of him. God knew all about it just as well when he first elected him, and yet, moved by his own motives of love, mercy, and wisdom, he did elect him, foreknowing all his possible meanness.

(c), The same conclusion follows from God's covenant of redemption with his Son the Messiah. This was a compact made from eternity between the Father and the Son. In this the Son freely bound himself to die for the sins of the world and to fulfil his other offices as Mediator for the redemption of God's people. God covenanted on this condition to give to his Son this redeemed people as his recompense. In this covenant of redemption Christ furnished and fulfilled the whole conditions; his redeemed people none. So, when Christ died, saying "It is finished," the compact was finally closed; there is no room, without unfaithfulness in the Father, for the final falling away of a single star out of our Saviour's purchased crown; read John xvii. It is "an everlasting covenant, ordered in all things, and is sure." (2 Sam. xxiii. 5.)

(d), We must infer the same blessed truth from Christ's love in dying for his people while sinners, from the supreme merits of his imputed righteousness, and the power of his intercession: "God commendeth his love toward us, in that, while we were yet sinners, Christ died for us. For if, when we were enemies, we were reconciled to God by the death of his Son, much more, being reconciled, we shall be saved by his life." (Rom. v. 8–10.)   "He that spared not his own Son, but delivered him up for us all, how shall he not with him also freely give us all things?" (Rom. viii. 32.)   Of Christ, the Intercessor, it is said: "Him the Father heareth always."   But see John xvii. 20: "Neither pray I for these alone, but for them also which shall believe on me through their word."   If the all-prevailing High Priest prays for all believers, all of them will receive what he asks for.   But what and how much does he ask for them?   Some temporary, contingent and mutable grace, contingent on the changeable and fallible human will?   See John xvii. 24: "Father, I will that they also whom thou hast given me be with me where I am; that they may behold my glory, which thou hast given me."

(e), If any man is converted, it is because the Ho'y Ghost is come into him; if any sinner lives for a time the divine life, it is because the Holy Ghost is dwelling in him.   But the Bible assures us that this Holy Ghost is the abiding seed of spiritual life, the earnest of heaven, and the seal of

our redemption.* Believers are "born by the word of God, of a living and incorruptible seed, which abideth and liveth forever." The Apostle Paul declares† that they receive the earnest of the Spirit, and that his indwelling is "the earnest of the purchased possession."‡ The same apostle says (Eph. iv. 30): "Grieve not the Holy Spirit of God, whereby ye are sealed unto the day of redemption."

An earnest, or earnest-money, is a smaller sum paid in cash when a contract is finally closed, as an unchangeable pledge that the future payments shall also be made in their due time. A seal is the final imprint added by the contracting parties to their names to signify that the contract is closed and binding. Such is the sanctifying presence of the Holy Spirit in every genuine be-

---

* See I John iii. 9 : "Whosoever is born of God doth not commit sin ; for his seed remaineth in him: and he cannot sin, because he is born of God."

† 2 Cor. i. 22 : "Who hath also sealed us, and given the earnest of the Spirit in our hearts." 2 Cor. v. 5 : "Now he that hath wrought us for the selfsame thing is God, who also hath given unto us the earnest of the Spirit."

‡ Eph. i. 14: "Which is the earnest of our inheritance until the redemption of the purchased possession, unto the praise of his glory."

liever; a deathless principle of perseverance therein, God's advanced pledge of his purpose to give heaven also, God's seal affixed to his covenant of grace. This, then, is the blessed assurance of hope which the true believer is privileged to attain: not only that God is pledged conditionally to give me heaven, provided I continue to stick to my gospel duty in the exercise of my weak, changeable, fallible will. A wretched consolation that to the believer who knows his own heart! But the full assurance of hope is this: Let the Holy Spirit once touch this dead heart of mine with his quickening light, so that I embrace Christ with a real penitent faith; then I have the blessed certainty that "this God who hath begun the good work in me, will perfect it unto the day of Jesus Christ" (his judgment day),* that the same divine love will infallibly continue with me notwithstanding subsequent sins and provocations, will chastise, restore, and uphold me, and give me the final victory over sin and death. This is the hope inexpressible and full of glory, a thousand-fold better adapted to stimulate in me obedience, the prayer, the watchfulness, the striv-

---

* Phil. i. 6 : " Being confident of this very thing, that he which hath begun a good work in you will perform *it* until the day of Jesus Christ."

ing, which are the means of my victory, than the
chilling doubts of possible falling from grace.
Again, the Scriptures are our best argument. I
append a few texts among many: See Jer. xxxii.
40 : "And I will make an everlasting covenant
with them, that I will not turn away from them,
to do them good; but I will put my fear in their
hearts, *that they shall not depart from me.*" *My
sheep never perish*, and none shall pluck them out
of my hand.* 2 Tim. ii. 19 : " The foundation of
God standeth sure, having this seal, the Lord
knoweth them that are his." Christ himself im-
plies that it is not possible to deceive his elect:†
1 Peter i. 5 : Believers "are kept by the power of
God through faith unto salvation." The same apostle thus explains the apostasy of final backsliders.
2 Peter ii. 22 : "The sow that was washed returns
to her wallowing in the mire." She is a sow still
in her nature, though with the outer surface
washed, but never changed into a lamb; for if she
had been, she would never have chosen the mire.

---

* John x. 27 : " My sheep hear my voice and I know
them, and they follow me. "

† Matt. xxiv. 24: " For there shall arise false Christs,
and false prophets, and shall shew great signs and won-
ders ; insomuch that, if *it were* possible, they shall deceive the very elect."

The apostle (1 John ii. 19) explains final back-slidings in the same way, and in words which simply close the debate: "They went out from us, but they were not of us; for if they had been of us, they would no doubt have continued with us; but they went out that they might be made manifest that they were not all of us."

My affirmative argument virtually refutes all objections. But there are two to which I will give a word. Arminians urge always an objection drawn from their false philosophy. They say that if God's grace in regeneration were efficient, cer-tainly determining the convert's will away from sin to gospel duty, it would destroy his free-agency. Then there would be no moral nor de-serving quality in his subsequent evangelical obe-dience to please God, any more than in the natu-ral color of his hair, which he could not help. My answer is, that *their philosophy is false.* The presence and operation of a right principle in a man, certainly determining him to right feelings and actions, does not infringe his free-agency but rather is essential to all right free-agency. My proofs are, that if this spurious philosophy were true, the saints and elect angels in heaven could not have any free-agency or praise-worthy character or conduct. For they are certainly and

forever determined to holiness.   The man Jesus
could not have had any free-agency or merit, for
his human will was absolutely determined to holiness.   God himself could not have had any freedom or praiseworthy holiness.   He least of all!
for his will is eternally, unchangeably, and necessarily determined to absolute holiness.   If there
is anything approaching blasphemy in this, take
notice, it is not mine.   I put this kind of philosophy from me with abhorrence.

    It is objected, again, that the Bible is full of
warnings to believers to watch against apostasy,
like this in 1 Cor. x. 12: "Let him that thinketh
he standeth take heed lest he fall."   The sophism
is, that if believers cannot fall from grace all these
warnings are absurd.   I reply, they are reasonable, because believers could fall from grace if they
were left to their own natural powers.   In this
sense, they naturally might fall, and therefore
watchfulness is reasonably urged upon them, because God's unchangeable purpose of grace towards them is effectuated in them, not as if they
were stocks or stones, or dumb beasts, *but
rational free agents, to be guided and governed by
the almighty Spirit through the means of rational
motives.*   Therefore, when we see God plying
believers with these rational motives not to back-

slide, it is not to be inferred that he secretly intends to let them backslide fatally, but rather just the contrary. I will close with a little parable: I watch a wise, intelligent, watchful, and loving mother, who is busy about her household work. There is a bright little girl playing about the room, the mother's darling. I hear her say, "take care, baby dear, don't go near that bright fire, for you might get burned." Do I argue thus? Hear that woman's words! I infer from them that that woman's mind is made up to let that darling child burn itself to death unless its own watchfulness shall suffice to keep it away from the fire, the caution of an ignorant, impulsive, fickle little child. What a heartless mother! But I do not infer thus, unless I am a heartless fool. I know that this mother knows the child is a rational creature, and that rational cautions are one species of means for keeping it at a safe distance from the fire; therefore she does right to address such cautions to the child; she would not speak thus if she thought it were a mere kitten or puppy dog, and would rely on nothing short of tying it by the neck to the table leg. But I also know that that watchful mother's mind is fully made up that the darling child shall not burn itself at this fire. If the little one's impulsiveness and short memory cause it to neglect the maternal cautions, I know that I shall see that good woman instantly drop her instruments of labor and *draw back her child with physical force from that fire*, and then most rationally renew her cautions to the child as a reasonable agent with more emphasis. And if the little one proves still heedless and wilful, I shall see her again rescued by physical force, and at last I shall see the mother impressing her cautions on the child's mind more effectually, perhaps by passionate caresses, or perhaps by a good switching, both alike the expressions of faithful love.

Such is the Bible system of grace which men call Calvinism, so often in disparagement. Its least merit is that it corresponds exactly with experience, common sense, and true philosophy. Its grand evidence is that it corresponds with Scripture. "Let God be true, and every man a liar." This doctrine exalts God, his power, his sovereign, unbought love and mercy. They are entitled to be supremely exalted. This doctrine humbles man in the dust. He ought to be humbled; he is a guilty, lost sinner, the sole, yet the certain architect of his own ruin. Helpless, yet guilty of all that makes him helpless, he ought to take his place in the deepest contrition, and give all the glory of his redemption to God. This doctrine, while it lays man's pride low, gives him an anchor of hope, sure and steadfast, drawing him to heaven; for his hope is founded not in the weakness, folly, and fickleness of his human will, but in the eternal love, wisdom, and power of almighty God. "O Israel, who is like unto thee, O people saved by the Lord!" "The eternal God is thy refuge, and underneath are the everlasting arms." (Deut xxxiii. 29, 27.)

RELATED SOLID GROUND TITLES

Classic Reformed Discourses & Essays by J.H.M. D'Aubigne
Seventeen classic Reformed essays, discourses and homilies
by the brilliant and godly Swiss Reformed Pastor-historian.
"His writing breathes sincerity and truth; his defense of the
gospel is profound and erudite; his love for its defenders is
infectious. The articles in this volume are sure to bring glory to
God and true spiritual pleasure to his saints." - Tom J. Nettles

The Word and Prayer: Classic Devotions from the Minor Prophets -
John Calvin compiled by Charles E. Edwards
"...will prove a welcome aid to the cultivation of Christian
piety, as well as public prayer." - Ligon Duncan

Calvinism in History: A Political, Moral & Evangelizing Force
Nathaniel S. McFetridge
"I do not know of any other book that sets forth so effectively
and yet in such a brief form the real nature of Calvinism and
the effect that it has had in history." Loraine Boettner
"This is a readable and happy account of Calvinism in
history." Rousas Rushdoony
"This book sure-footedly guides us over the terrain of Calvinism's
broad-sweeping political and moral influence, concluding that
Calvinism's evangelistic power results from the doctrines of grace,
particularly justification by faith alone." Joel Beeke

Call us Toll Free at 1-877-666-9469
Visit us on the web at solid-ground-books.com

Other Solid Ground Titles

Printed in the United States
70994LV00001B/46-243